FOR Margaret

The Knife in the Wave

MARY O'MALLEY

With appreciation

Mary O'Malley.

salmonpoetry

First published in 1997 by
Salmon Publishing Ltd.,
Cliffs of Moher, Co. Clare
Website: www.salmonpoetry.com
emaill: info@salmonpoetry.com
Reprinted in 1997 & 2001 by Salmon Publishing Ltd.

A catalogue record for this book is available from the British Library.

The Arts Council
An Chomhairle Ealaíon

Salmon Publishing gratefully acknowledges the
financial assistance of the Arts Council.

ISBN 1 897648 87 1 Paperback

Cover design by Estresso
Set by Siobhán Hutson
Printed by Offset Paperback Mfrs., PA

In memory of my father,
Padhraic O'Malley

Acknowledgements

Acknowledgements are due to the editors of the following, where some of these poems first appeared: *Poetry Ireland Review, The Southern Review, Anthology of the University of Michigan at Ann Arbor, The Years Best Fantasy and Horror, Windows, The Atlanta Review, Seneca Review.*

Several of the poems in this collection have been broadcast on RTE Radio, RTE Television, and BBC Radio.

Special thanks to The Arts Council, The Tyrone Guthrie Centre at Annaghmakerrig, L'Imaginaire Irlandais, and RTE Television which commissioned 'The Joe Heaney Poems'.

Anois an t-am don rince aonair
ar ghainimh bheo na trá –
na chosa a chaitheamh go háiféiseach
is leá d'aonghnó sa teas.

Better rise up now, a solo-dancer,
on the hot sands of the strand,
throw out both legs, at random,
and melt down in the sun.

– Seán ó Tuama, 'Besides, Who Knows Before
    The End, What Light May Shine'

Contents

Meditation On The Long Walk

Desire would be a simple thing,
All those Gods rampant
And the earth moving for Leda;
Her life transformed by his seed,
What was engendered revealed
The mystery of what she understood
Economically preserved
In a ripple of uncluttered hindsight.

Flip the coin and let the wives out.
Yeats' telling questions hang
Upside down like fish-hooks
Or inverted swans' necks. With her beak
Savage at his loins
Indifferent to all but his seed
Is there talk of ecstacy and knowledge
Among the tumbling feathers?

Yet there is an attractive symmetry,
That lust without responsibility
She peeled back to pure desire
Him a real God, the earth
Pulsing briefly like a star
And a few thousand years away
A poet trawling the night sky
For a single blinding metaphor.

The Annunciation

History is teeming with comely maidens
Awaiting godly transformations.

Leda, Yourself and the Conneely girl
Must have felt the same fear

When used as host
By swan, merman and Holy Ghost.

This given, did He have to send
Such a fey announcing angel round

With a mouth like a jaded sex tourist,
Or is this where God bows to the artist?

All three know the transformation
From luscious girl to Pietà

Pregnant, on the run, crucified with tears
Will take three months less than thirty-four years,

That you will then bear nineteen centuries
Of prayers for airports, intercession, cures.

Did a trace of that plundered innocence
Tint the rose windows of Notre Dame with radiance?

Here, where people carried knives
Between them and marauding spirits

When they sang your lament in triplicate
In words familiar and intimate

The litany of limb and feature by destroyed mothers
Stopped the hand of Gods and artists.

Innocentii

They are not here – clay never held them
But it is entirely possible
That they return to consecrate this place,
Bless their fathers' avid eyes, fill
The universe of their mothers' arms,
Wise as quatrocento angels.

Look for them in slanted light.
A host as soft as mothwings swoops and dips
Across the bay. They are up after bedtime
Retouching the lake with gleam and glint,
Tossing the Clare hills to desert,
Dimpling the sea. In this time of wonders
It is entirely possible
That we are islands in the territory of angels.

*This poem is carved in limestone in the burial ground
for unbaptised infants in Galway.*

Interior

'There is no domestic detail in her poems …'

There is now. Two by fours
And concrete slabs, the floors
Littered with cigarette stubs.

The timber supporting the new stairs
Is stalwart. 'That won't shift.'
It will of course and its all useless

When the electrician's mate
Kangoes through the live wire
Playing a mean guitar.

Good golly, Miss Molly. 'Draw a straight line
Up from the switch, in your mind.
That's called an image.' I told him

But they're only interested in grouting
And gulley risers, a consonance of solid things.
Nuts and bolts men.

The skin of ochre paint in the bedroom
Has done more to hold this house together
Than a gross of six inch nails.

'There's a fault in the living-room walls.
It could be the wrong shade of red – Atomic Flash.'
Like Gods, they never listen.

Forgive Me That I Am Coping Badly

After Akhmatova

There is no use bringing politics into it,
I would have coped as badly in any gender
At times like this, with breath pinched
To show that it is rationed,
Words rioting on all sides
And my cinnamon daughter
Spreading honey on my final, final manuscript.
What has happened to my organised life
When disaster was 'Saturday night
And not a child in the house washed'?

A Touch of Sass

Once I saw a black woman with sass
Conducting English like a big band,
Words danced and a jazz chant
Two-stepped across the floor.
Sounds rocked and rolled, vowels
Stretched and yawned and sighed
As Maya Angelou put some revolution
In the elocution class.
I closed my eyes and smiled
And thought of England.

Song of the Wise Woman

Speak to me of tapestry
Speak to me of gold
Speak to me
Of a flowering tree
Watered by a woman's blood.

Read to me of hanging stars
Read to me of love
Read me that dark talking tree
That hides a secret child.

Sing away the dark man's touch
For I am still and cold
Sing me air and sing me fire
With your voice of wintery gold.

Whisper me a legend
Whisper me a lie
Whisper me a flowering tree
And warm me in its fire.

Weave me in your tapestry
Thread me through with gold
But I must tend the Winter tree
Watered by a woman's blood.

Sarajevo String Quartet

Imagine carnage in the marketplace,
Young women traded for chocolates,
The lash and recoil on an old man's face
When he is offered the price of two packs
Of Marlboro for his wife's wedding ring.
You cannot. Overkill blankets Sarajevo.

A musician stands beside the empty stalls
Like an elongated question mark.
He appears, unshaven and pale – the details
Do not matter. As he plants his instrument
Place two fingers at your throat. That's better.
Imagine the first bow stroke.
Whatever he plays will be a requiem.
Now listen, the slow timbery notes of the cello.

Starfish

for Grainne Pollack

Pale wanton little dancer
She floats through life,
Meat to every dead-eyed predator.
Those soft limbs deceive.
Dizzy with night phosphorous
She wheels and spindrifts,
Aching to propel
The whole flung-out joy of her
Into the breath-held sky.

The Priest's Mistress' Tale

He seeks her out on gala nights
when she shines – they are good together then,
more than the sum of their parts.

They meet in hotels by open fires
for evenings of books and talk,
ambered in one another's lives.

In between they are far planets
separately busy in cold space.
They keep the rules of a Descartian universe.

When they make love the stars misbehave
all over the sky. Sadly he tells her
'We are bespoke.' Like overcoats, or graves.

Untitled

She is irrevocably growing
towards the light, moving
into a room of her own, the attic.
Strong at last, she should feel triumphant.

Instead, her head is bent
to the slow pipe notes of lament.
These are the loneliest steps
this side of the grave.

She would give it all for the impossible,
Him to come with her.

The Wound

Nothing changes. The legend tells of three men
In a currach, fishing.
A big sea rose up and threatened to engulf them.

They cast lots to see who was wanted – a young man.
As the swell hung over him
He grabbed a knife and pitched in desperation,

Cold steel against the wave.
The sea withdrew and all were saved.
One man heard a cry of pain and prayed.

At nightfall a woman on a white horse
Enquired and found the house.
'My mistress is sick and only you can save her,'

She said and gave him guarantees.
They took the road under the sea
To a palace where a beautiful woman lay.

His knife was buried in her right breast.
'This is the knife you cast into my flesh.
You must pull it out with a single stroke

Or I will die by midnight.' He did
And the wound became a rose. She offered
The treasures of her green underworld,

A pagan kiss. The same old story. She begged:
'This scar will ache forever if you go.'
Then a choir of lost men whispered

'Stay here and she will have your soul.'
So he blessed himself, refused and went above
To the simple solid world he understood.

Lullaby

Golden nets and silver fish
Floating in the sky,
Lift me on your shoulders Daddy,
Daddy swing me high.

And if the fishes are all tears
And if the nets are dry,
We'll chase the moon with blazing spears
Across the ice-cold sky.
Carry me on your shoulders Daddy,
Daddy swing me high.

Shoeing The Currach

Seventeen feet of canvas
Stretched across the supple hoops of her
And with one deft push of a shoe
She'd spin into his hands
And lightly he'd lift and turn her.

That's how it was with them
Until the balance shifted.
The foot smashed down,
An awkward turn, he can't hold her,
Now she's torn and useless on the sand.

Disgusted, he walks away,
His big hands useless
And no words for what is done.

A Young Matron Dances Free of the Island

One Tuesday in November she finished the wash-up,
Mounted a white horse
And rode into the force nine waves
Out beyond the lighthouse.
Feck it, she said, startling the neighbours,
It's go now or be stuck here forever
Chained to this rock like that Greek,
With the gannets tearing at my liver.

She rode bareback out the roads. The horse reared
But climbed the foothills of the breakers.
When she heard her children calling
Mama, mama, she turned, praying
Jesus, let me make shore
And I will never desert them again,
Nor be ungrateful. When she got in
Half drowned, there was no-one there.

For weeks in the psychiatric all she could see
Were graveyards, men laid out in coffins,
The little satin curtains
They would have shunned in life, of palest ivory
About to be drawn. It was the long winters
They say, drove her out again
To where there was no going back.
She loved parties, was a beautiful dancer –

There is no other explanation.
The husband was good to her, by all accounts.
Does it matter? There should be a moment,
A shard of glass to hold against the light,
A checkpoint to pass before the end.
He has nothing, though people are kind.
They say her hair caught the sun
As she waltzed over the cliff, haloing beautifully down.

Ceasefire

The North has shifted.
I run to the telephone, excited

As when I used to show him
My pet mice in a sweet jar, grooming.

Between the thought
And the instrument I stop

Blinded. No-one else in the world
Would be as glad.

A word drops between us – dead
Blunt as an iron half-hundredweight.

Barcarole

The black boat is pushed out.
And will not come back.
Between here and South America
She will sail into the white roses
From the feast of the virgin of Guadaloupe.
O Mhaighdean, bear him with tenderness.
Hold his hand in the dark places.

The Otter Woman

i

Against the wisdom of shore women
She stood on the forbidden line too long
And crossed the confluence of sea and river.
One shake of her body on O'Brien's bridge
And the sea was off her.
A glorious swing from haunch to shoulder
Sent water arching in the sunlight,
A fan of small diamonds flicked open,
Held, fell. Her smooth pelt rose into fur.

He stood and watched her from the shadows
And moved to steal her tears
Scattered on the riverbank.
Now he could take his time. He smoked.

She was all warm animal following the river,
Trying her new skin like a glove.
He trailed her, magnetised by her power to transform,
The occasional bliss on her face, her awakened body.
Once or twice she saw him.
Her instincts were trusting on land.
They smiled. This took the whole Summer.

He took her by a lake in Autumn
A sliced half moon and every star out
The plough ready to bite the earth.

She left him on a street corner
With no choice and no glance back,
Spring and a bomber's moon.
In between their loosed demons
Played havoc in the town.

He pinned her to the ground, his element.
This was not what she came for
But what she got.
Soon the nap of her skin rose only for him.
It was too late to turn back.
She grew heavy out of water.

ii

Indifferent to all but the old glory
He never asked why she always walked
By the shore, what she craved,
Why she never cried when every wave
Crescendoed like an orchestra of bones.

She stood again on the low bridge
The night of the full moon.
One sweet deep breath and she slipped in
Where the river fills the sea.
She saw him clearly in the street light – his puzzlement.
Rid of him she let out
One low strange cry for her human sacrifice,
For the death of love
For the treacherous undertow of the tribe
And dived, less marvellous forever in her element.

Miss Panacea Regrets

for Ann Gibbons

'Give in! Don't you know no one escapes
the power of creatures reaching out with
breath alone?'

    Marina Tsvetayeva

i

I have lost May but it surfaces here.
Each time a breath lifts it from the page
it rises, a moon gleaming like an old sixpence.

They have pierced my breast.
The wound, unstitched, blossomed
and like Philoctetes I am unhealed.
All that lovely month I limped on half-sail,
half-life in the rose scented mornings,
A hot-house virgin on a May altar.

Yes, there are shafts of pain
Dark and no-one knows their depth.
Is there no-one to burn for me like a black candle?
Who dares to pray?
Marina, I would hold your pain
but who would contain mine?
It rages through the dawn
blazing the lyric down
and blackening all the hawthorn.

My pain is hungry and lean.
It licks the skin, eats shame slowly
and wolfs through to the bone
but the real work, the slow burn
is in the sinews, like a poem.
That's what the man said – a bit slight
but sinewy all the same. Not tough enough, I felt.
The wolf is tearing at my chest.

Men with knives surround me.
It is half past one.
They will come at two
for the third time to cut into my chest
and release a thousand roses.
The instructions – between the fourth
and fifth ribs – are precise.
It is all done without screaming,
without making a fuss.
I am not brave. 'I can't.'
It is my own thin voice.
I have no shame, no control.

You will not stitch breath
with such blunt instruments.
Use salve, some unguent made with herbs.
Pray to Hygeia, Apollo, Panacea
For a drug to help us tolerate
the mercury heavy air.

A youth in a white coat walks away.
He has stitched in the uncoiling thorns.
He is a climber bagging peaks.
Pain is not his business –
not quantifiable like the carcass.
Is that Shylock peeking around the screen
And Polonius behind the arras?
The colour of St. Teresa's ward is hideous.
My husband comforts me.
A nurse holds me down.

22

I have been betrayed and time
is an altered state. It coils and flattens
like a sea snake.
The days of the dead
follow. I know I am dead and there is nowhere
else to go, for ever and ever amen.
I am crying all night for my children.

Is there no-one to lay a head
against my torn breast and listen
to my ragged breathing?

What you hear with your stethoscope
Is not the true beat of her heart
Merely a counterpoint
to the rush and whisper of blood.

Not knowing this you say
This woman is afraid.
She craves sympathy.
With palms upturned when she has failed
To get better
You tell her, looking unconvinced,
'We are not God'.
She knows, but sometimes
You are all there is.

They have pierced my breast.
The double edge of doctor's hands
Squeeze from me the strangled inhalation
of birth. When the pain subsides
there is a shudder, a child's endless desolation.
It is dangerous to let
all the grieving women
loose like this. They could drown you
in their funeral sighs.

I am small and broken on an iron bed
anchored in the Regional Hospital
where they mostly do what they can
but brook no talk of pain. Its implements
are too blunt, the sledgehammer,
the jagged glass,
the drops of molten lead. It is all rack
and ruin here after midnight.
An island woman moans.
This, she says, is not my real face.
Lady Morphia sneers and walks away
with her white coat open
and her black hair loose.

I flounder in a storm of wasted breath :
The times I didn't dance a requiem waltz
for the forgotten dead,
my chastised children's tears,
the forbidden noun of a name
launched into the waiting night
is lost in the wake
of the poem not spoken, the prayer not said.
I could end this voyage
with my keel on top yet.

They have pierced my flesh.

The wolf is snarling at my bed.
He never leaves me – when I sleep
His low growl tatters the edge of my dreams.
I tell my children it's a dog
that only barks because he is afraid.
Soon he will go away.
They are unconvinced
by this American psychology.

I am tired. A friend will emerge
to ring the hospital with silver bells.
(And garlic, she quips, for Doctor Death).
There will be red and purple roses
raging at dawn and in the end there will be time
to say the long magnificat
or not. Mind me. I am tired.
All that ancient grief chokes me.
There is lead in my veins.
Let me sleep. I am tired
keeping planes up,
high buildings from falling on my children,
fending the dragons that enter my room,
feeding the dragons that hold up the moon.

Look, someone has brought delphiniums.
Their blue closes over me, cool as peace.

ii

Lady Morphia enters.
This time she is a woman my own age.
'I will control your pain,' she says,
'This, after all, is nineteen ninety two'
and busies herself with needles
the way certain women do. I cry
short jerky tears. A hand on my shoulder
welcomes me to Mercy street.
My words of thanks tear like asbestos.

A black Homer is salving
incurable wounds in the No Pain Café,
He has fashioned me a line
of perfect weightlessness to say.
I grasp this golden thread
and enter the labyrinth afraid.

. . . . A long pause.
One. Two. Three. Four
carries on, a metronome.
I enter gasping on the last beat
afraid as ever that a line
is measured by the breath.
The wolf is licking at my throat.

First the swelling bubble ... ooh.
I watch the sound grow,
a valley of echoes,
the sweet call of an island Homer,
the unheard birth cry of my daughter.
The poet's silver sheaves of light
are stooked above me in the dark.

I breathe.
In, out. In, out. I float
on the precise lightness of vowels.
Each one I exhale is faintly haloed
like a Czechoslovakian Christ.
The wolf is nuzzling at my throat.

It has been excised,
a weak spot in my breath
cut out and the tear stitched.
It is healing well. In time
it will become a faint mark,
my stolen language, an echo that tugs,
the need for a word not known
like grá or brón for love or pain.
Neither direct nor wrong.

They have changed my resonance,
stretched me tight as a drum.
Every ripple in the air plays me.
It is time to undertake
the rehabilitation of my voice,
the only instrument I play.
All that fire and ripped air
have cracked it.

It is retuned slowly,
the throat stretched,
the column of breath urged to my needs –
I have no patience
and worst of all no guarantee.
My own body
is making strange
like someone else's baby.

Poems like spears
pin me between earth and sky.
The moon sneers. In daylight
the sharp planes of colours
mean nothing will ever be as good
again and mean no more.
The coral sand in my fingers
grain on separate grain
is as undependable as the sun.
I know nothing of what this means
and all that can be said
is that no other world
would make Whitman roar
his grassy prayer
and the air holds power to cut or love me.

I have seen words made flesh,
whether poetry or delirium,
sanctuary lamps
that burned when the sun
quenched. Well, this is where it started,
the dark, every cell clenched, breath.
This time, diphthong before consonant.

Negative Numbers

for Oisín

Your son has not grasped
The concept of negative numbers
And you Ma'am, do not seem in the least perturbed.

No, Sir I'm not and he hasn't,
At least, Thank God, not yet.

The Lightcatchers

for Maeve on her eleventh birthday

St. Brigid's Day comes storming in,
I make my act of faith in Spring.
The mystery of planting – what grows
In bleak or lush places is on us.
A courgette swells from orange flowers
And the untilled rock yields sea thrift.

We reaped the wind and you came,
Child of hibiscus and cinnamon.
No statue from a cold museum
You spark and shine through every room
In the house. Home is the husk.
Soon you will shuck it off to go dancing.

Look how for centuries we nourished sons,
Buried the girl children, bound their feet.
Did we think it would make no difference?
As we slouch towards the millenium
The portents are all for the world ending.
Soldiers are sprouting along every border.
They are tumbling
Out of their mothers' wombs with guns.

Something has changed.
You are eleven this Saint Brigid's Day.
Last year's party girls in coloured dresses
Are swirling over our honey timbered floor,
A carousel of lightcatchers
Tinkling like Christmas chimes.
This year they will be more faceted still.
The music slows.

I hang a cross of fresh rushes.
There is a stretching under the ground,
A reaching for the sun.
Brid, open your throat and bless them!
Let this treasury of minded daughters
Planted as sapphires
Ripen across the continents into rubies.

The Sea Urchin

She needs the spines
For dignity, her natural resistance
Along faintly bruised lines.
Deep inside the shell she is exposed
And glows or shivers
In her soft pink flesh.
This is also where she cries
With her hundred crescent eyes.

Absent

Say mackerel shoaled through the lullabies
Wrens circled Christ's head and drank Mary's tears;
Say each love song was a festival of desire
And allow that the touch of some shapeless thing
Sickened his mind one night between bog and shore –
When he turned his back on his children
And cut their mother out of his life
He was harder than Connemara stone.

Old women pulled shawls over their faces
The silence of daughters descended
Our memories closed into a fist
And there was blood on the moon.

Couplets

Antidote

She set my task and daily dutiful
I contrive black and white unbeautiful

Lines. The first mistake was to read
Midsummer and become interested

In how the rhyming couplet
Purrs and stretches for Walcott.

This is, after all, a detox programme designed
To knock the prettiness out of my lines,

Toughen their hides, reduce simile
And bring the poison out in me.

Double

When you have crossed the equator,
Sailed down into that other hemisphere

I will reclaim every lane and alley
in the town. Footsteps will carry

back to the sixteenth century –
a woman's stealthy plunder, escape in a galley

slipped into the velvet town like a whisper.
With her world split open behind her

she stepped aboard without a word
and slid out the bay like a sword.

Down there under upside down stars
think of me. It will be safe.

When enough salt water has cleaned my wounds,
Feel my blessing sting your dreams.

Grainne's Comment On The Annalists

My match, O'Neill, Burke and Flaherty are gone.
I am up to my knees in small men.

They want a dried out virgin, a eunuch in skirts.
I wonder what they'll make of Eliza Beth

With their small appetites and big notions.
The belt and braces men of the emotions

Tire me. They'll write history? That's history's loss.
Let them decorate their little margins. Scribbling sea lice!

I've a good mind to set the peasants, cultured of course,
Loose on them and watch the sport

Or show that this pirate politically shrewd
Can still lose her temper and oblige with a sword.

What's the use? There is not even one dark
Enough to matter, or tamper with my heart.

I'm up to my knees in small men.
My match, O'Neill, Burke and Flaherty are gone.

Marina

Your name is a smooth green stone
Indented by the stroking of my thumb.

It is the first letter, a flaming word
Swelling out in echoes from the throat.

It is one of the secret signs
Between the wind and the seven seas.

Your name is a drink of spring water.
It is three candles lit on a bronze altar.

Funeral

It matters now, the funeral
A sign of age. The ritual

Lowering into the ground, the flat tamp
Of neighbours' spades on the earth.

Think of the jokes, a rosary of stories
Never to be refuted, flattering lies.

What is important is whether
The grave faces north or south. The weather

Should be stormy and above all, friends
Must not lie when they say 'At the end

She was peaceful
Though up to that she gave everyone hell.'

Twelve Holiday Home Lake

Has an o-one phone number
(Instead of an o nine five,)
Twelve pastel cow-sheds to sell
And a sewage tank
Beside the seven sisters well –
A telecommunications miracle.
The moral of the story is
Divine intervention
Aids planning permission
On the reservation or
Someone tied the right rag
On the right bush
And did alright in Dublin.

Knell

I want to write a simple poem
With the taste of green apple,
Clear as a high bell. A poem
Seamless as a grey chemise that fits
Like water, and not make a fuss for once,

But ordinary men are raping children
No older than my daughter.
They are invading their small bodies
Like missiles while Europe stares.
Every mother knows the way to stop them.

An old man is burning sticks
In the basement of the Europa hotel.
In the playing fields of Sarajevo
Goosesteps echo. A toddler,
His belly embroidered with shrapnel, screams.

I fear the cold silence of Europe.
It colours the apple's aftertaste,
Slows down the tune, prints seams of blood
On the silk. And all over Ireland
The bells are coming down.

The Assignation

'I'll meet you at the hotel at nine.
Failing that, or if you're late
We'll meet at the grave.
I've been thinking of what you should wear.
A dress,
Does that sound alright? 'Oh definitely.
No self-respecting Connemara woman
Would appear in a cemetery
In less.'

The Poor Clares

Admit me to the flickering company of women
That flame softly; let me see their tears,
Those made with a thirst rarely satisfied.
We are the handmaids of a stern Lord
Who led us to expect that he would one day bless
Our parched mouths with a holy kiss
And say 'You have passed the test.
Now I will mind you forever
And teach you the language of God.'
In that tongue we will converse
And be immortal. It is hard to live with any man
When she has longed for this.

La Nuit Étoilée

Not pretty. Whirlpools
    and sparking tops

Take fire
    from their own friction.

Beneath, a pair –
    lovers maybe, anyhow less significant

Than all those fireworks
    but still relevant

Are held
    like small dark moons

In their orbit,
    awed in a small way.

Your curse
    to be in no doubt

What symphony
    of mad airs

Above their heads
    being played out.

The Joe Heaney Poems

Famine Grass

He soaked it all in –
The generations of dead and banished
Had left words after them, chain-linked
From Rosmuc to Barna.
They waited to be voiced
Shivering in the folds of hills,
Leaning against gables,
Like old men, or drowned
At the mouth of every bay
From Bertraboy to Carna:
Famine grass, American wake, coffin-ship.
He said them among half-sets and jigs
And set Cearbhaill's love song
Wandering down the centuries.

Geis

I marked him young
And waited while he tended his book learning.
I watched him dig and grow strong,
Soon he could plane and polish a song.
He breathed deep and learned rhythm
Rowing currachs in the Carna sun.

He was a singer and the son of singers.
I let him play and led him to the well
When his wild days were over
I saw him drink with a bog thirst.
A thousand songs! Oh, he was fine
My young king of the sky.

London, Newport, Philadelphia, New York:
The path was laid out. All he had to do was sing.
His face became the perfect mask
For spirits older than a priest's blessing
To speak through and when he sang.
No other woman had a chance.

In return I put the burn of a turf fire,
The swish of a girl's bright skirt,
The ring of a horseshoe on stone in his voice.
In return, I was the woman with red hair
Watching his black eyes quench
When the last note snagged in his throat.

Yank Talk

A Connemara man? Tribesmen.
Oh, they can be fabulous.
That courtesy and charm
All the flair of a matador, and the skill.
They're dangerous, honey. Even in Brooklyn.
Don't you forget it.
And the women, Jesus!
They'll look at you like dirt.
He'll see exactly
What they're too polite to point out
And you'll always ask the wrong questions.
Assassination by conversation is how they do it.

He'll tease and tell you things
About your eyes –
When all the coaxing eases off
And the compliments end
They don't talk. Never again.
They sing though and tell stories
Of how the west was won and lost,
And lost. You know the worst?
They only ever really fall for boats.

Caoineadh Mhaire

Why do we love men that are bad for us –
Are we that weak? Hardly the kisses,
Fruit in the mouth soon melts.
His Spaniard's eyes never settled on me right
But the mouth music lured me.

There was something old about his voice
That took the city ground from under me
And brought little yellow shells
Scattering up the back streets of Glasgow.
Oh he was handsome, though, like a stag.

When I felt the fine sand
Between my toes I should have run
To the nearest forgettable city boy
And chanced the ordinary,
But he sang and I was caught.

I listened as the hook eased in,
Listened for the blás* he put on my name
Until all I could hear was my own breath
Like the tide in a cave, echoing, going out
And the children crying.

A grey crow settled on my chest
And took his time.
A high price for a slow song:
'A Pheadair, a Aspail, an bhfaca tu mo ghrá bhán?
Ochon agus ochon o.' ★★

★ *blás – accent. Literally translates as taste or relish.*
★★ *These lines are a refrain from the Lament of the Three Virgins, based on
a twelfth century European song, which is still sung in Ireland. The Irish title
is Caoineadh na dTrí Mhuire.*

Man to Man, The Angels Converse

Go on, whisper.
What do you really think of women?
I saw you looking at that blonde
And her making eyes for attention.
I saw you looking past her
Like a sheik.

Did you ever trust a woman
Either lover or wife or whore,
Apart from your mother? You can tell me.
I am the guardian of the half door
And between the two of us
They are all soft and secretive
As a bed of sin, out to tame a man
And clip his wings. Come on now, confess.
Do you believe a woman has a soul
The same as us?

Footsteps

Christ, a man is dogged from cradle to grave.
First it was my own steps
Behind me on the Carna road
Coming late from a dance.

Thrown out of college for a cigarette
I met my father's coffin on the way home,
Sunday shoes on the gravelly path.
I quickstepped back to Dublin.

Before the bog could suck me in
Or the sea swallow me I went
To plough the rocks of foreign cities
With unshed songs and my bare hands,

My cardboard suitcase
Tied with string, an address in Southampton
On the back of a cigarette pack:
'Flow gently, sweet Afton, among thy green braes ... '

Look. I am the custodian of our songs.
I know the highest note permitted,
The longest line, the way the voice
Should settle in the throat.

Maybe Glasgow was a mistake. I left
With children pounding in my head and a wife.
Christ. I crossed the Atlantic and never looked back.
When you sing all else is silenced.

America, where the past ends six inches below
The asphalt. For years I left it all behind.
Then I heard them in New York, the old men
My teachers, shuffling on forty-second street.

Footsteps. They gather in the dark and swell
Like applause. Soon I will close my ears to all
But the little silver heel taps that have rung
Around my head like tuning forks

In the long silence, the pause before the living join
The slow processional circling of the dead.

The Seal Woman

for Maureen Kenny

> ' … *And the best thing about the legend is*
> *I can enter it anywhere. And have.'*
>
> Eavan Boland, *The Pomegranate*

Prologue

In the after midnight quiet
A dislodged volume of Homer tumbles to the floor.
The noise brings the racket of departed builders
Echoing back. Relief, then silence reassembles. I sit
And lock the glass doors that will eventually fill
The space kangoed through the block wall
Into the kitchen. Was it worth the fuss?
I am working late to assemble tools
And impose some small order
On the chaos of books and dust.
I draw a blank page across my desk
And in its white wake, words,
Perhaps some phrases shaken from the falling epic,
Swirl and collide, then sink.
A sound such as extinguishing stars
Might make draws me to the window.

i

It begins here
With a couple uncoupled on a beach.
He is misnaming the constellations,
Stumbling through the Pleiades, content.
He smokes a cigarette and stretches.
She is standing waiting on the sea.
He fails to notice the caul steal over her eyes.
He lacks imagination or, be charitable,
It could be that his sight is blurred by passion.
Who is she and what has reduced her to this,
Shape-changing beside a man who doesn't notice?

I do not want them in my new room.
They intrude and clutter
My attempt at order.
They threaten to invite the moon
Of whose round vowels I have had enough
To stare in through my open window.
They are not alone of course – the whole cast
And backdrop of their story
Crowds into my study –
Even fictive lovers must have an audience.

There are mermaids from St Nicholas' cathedral
Assorted architects and developers,
A reverend mother and the banned ghost
Of Grainne Mhaol. Is she heading for a ball

Or up to no good? She is cloaked and masked.
Diverse sea virgins and convent girls
Mysterious city fathers,
And Tyrannosaurus JCB, the pride of the parade.A
Claddagh man, a boatbuilder by trade
Will have no part in this outlandish procession.

Absence is his vantage point.
Then the seal-woman and a man who eats fire
But is himself cold, a chessmaster and liar.

They might at least tell me their names.
It would be handy to know which goddess
She is in advance of the action
And what to call inaction-man relaxing by the ocean.

The set is granite with an arch,
Dressed stone walls, stark
Lines smudged and broken by water –
One false step and you're in the river.
Now all is laid open for the tawdry
Assault of the pastel merchants
Ready with paint and balcony.

That Spring tide the water level rose.
Flood Street was awash and in Salthill
The tide slipped across the prom
Lapping the walkers' ankles.
The Claddagh man has noticed an increase in seals.
They gather daily outside the otter's window,
One is always separate.
She had loved a man and, so the story goes
Was lonely for her own people. She left
But her world was dim without him.
She has come to bring him home.

Under the fisherman's tower
The seal woman surfaces.
She draws her body up onto the bank
For the second time. Every fibre stretches and wracks.
She cries and heaves towards the city.
Tears scald her eyes and fall as glass.

'I remember those old walls, flesh satisfying swords,
The power of curses.' Another breath and she drags forward.
She cuts a face into the rock with a diamond tear
Fingers it like a familiar continent, softly swears.

A dark man,
Walks the streets oblivious, but not innocent.
He leads a charmed life.

Once, a wino died beside him in the street,
A woman disintegrated like plate glass
And a car exploded. He walked on
Talking about the North, the children he would have,
His next building,
And strolled through streets

Teeming with happy drunks and lovers
And smiled and kissed her mouth
Oblivious to the scars
That flowered open on her breast.
This much she remembers.

She is growing lighter. The sun is honey on her throat.
She risks a deeper breath and tries her first note –
It grates. She sings again, a note of such sweetness
The little mermaids smile and scuttle down
From windows and doorways
Where they have perched for three hundred years,
Loitering with intent.

iii

In Galvia, a town founded on a wake
That started for a Prince's daughter
And hasn't stopped yet,
The mermaids on window and footstone shift,
The Clontuskert woman closes her book,
The St. Nicholas girls pack
Combs and mirrors in their purses.

The bold-faced one on the church's north aisle
Intends heading to Grealy's for lipstick.
She'll throw off her tail like a gymslip
And strut her stuff the length of Shop Street
Got up in a mini-skirt and high heels.
She can't wait to get rid of all that hair
In a spiky cut and be a Quay Street angel.

The county club mermaid has no context.
This disturbs the archaeologist.
Her greed and lust are not, in this case
Balanced by good. She is deposed,
Temptation's sister,
Three centuries out of kilter,
Taken from her window to a doorstop.

'This town is done for,' the Claddagh man says.
'It is drowning in blue triangles and pink portholes.
One of these days, it will get what it deserves.'

Next morning, salt water trickles through
The basement of Kenny's bookshop
Where old beams have held the building up
Since fourteen seventy-two.

★   *The mermaids referred to are figures on St. Nicholas' Collegiate Church
Galway, the County Club, and the west doorway of a fifteenth century priory
at Clontuskert, Co. Galway.*

iv

A high note shivers over the water,
A snatch of Monteverdi's erotic madrigal.
Her lover hears it and is enchanted.
Soon, there is faint vibration
From the far side of the bridge.
The signature of his footsteps becomes a tune
Under the whine and thrum of car engines,
The thud and tap of pedestrians.
He is entering the town, cocksure.
He pauses and lights a cigarette, draws the fire in.
She peels off her gloves
And hides them in an interstice of the Spanish Arch,
Grey sealskin.

She cuts her eyes at the pink whore, a building
On the bank. The gulls are restless.
Her chest, a tortured honeycomb,
Expands slowly. The fossilised skeleton of a boat
Invites rest. She sits.
Here Columbus took stock and headed west
With his sextant and other men's instruments.

A gull swoops in, the river shines.
her skin is a bed of fresh herbs in the evening.
The blood, coursing through her veins
Bubbles like champagne. She is newly born,
Radiant. She draws the air deep into her lungs.

She sees a hooker sailing past the statue of liberty
And crawling along a jet's flight path
A ship with skeletons in the rigging
Slices the sky open and disappears into a gap
Which closes along the scar of the plane's track –
The two-thirty from Shannon
Bound for Boston and half an hour late.

'I remember slipping out the bay like a whisper.
Star and mark and tide obeyed my navigator's hand.
'Ne O ne Mac shall strut ne swagger
Through the streets of Galway.' Once clear, I laughed.'

His cigarette glows as he leans at ease
Over the parapet.
Once when he kissed her
She could breathe in the stars.
They entered her lungs, were purified
And imparted heat to her blood.
She breathed out a vowel of pure flame, love.
Now they are figures on an old vase.

v

You can enter the legend anywhere.
On High Street a man is being measured up
For a bainin jacket in Molloy's shop.
There are bolts of swansdown and muslin.
Outside the streets are emptying.

All evening she wanders the estates
Waiting for the moon to rise.
She looks in on an old school friend
Presses her face against the windowpane
And sees her reading to her children.

She looks with envy at the settled women
Gossiping by the fire.
They make lovely pictures
With husbands and garnet wine,
Candles shattering the crystal.
She would like to join them
But what would she have to talk about?

She knows ordinary women
Half love normal men.
They learn survival, a lukewarm thing,
But this revenge is cold.
For years she scarcely thought of them.
Now it is far too late.

She cups the young moon between her palms
And makes to draw it down. One by one
Hard diamonds glitter in the sky,
Incalculably cold. Look, he once said annoyed,
What the fuck are the stars for anyway?

To be saved there is a task she must perform.
The knives are sharpening in her eyes.
She must shine one more time for him,
Outdo herself this once,
Release the last drops of light
Stored in the amber at her throat.
Then she would bring him down and quench.

vi

A red sun hissed as she struck out.
Her heels clicked on the bridge,
To her left, fish or knife blades flashed
Then flicked over the weir.
Her stride lengthened, the ends of her skirt
Caught fire – the last of the sunset.

The city's poor, the mullet children scavenging,
Stopped to stare. Baggypants, bigshirt,
At the convent railings
They swigged booze and swore.
A girl, her eyes glazed in ecstacy,
Swung out into her path,
Then swirled back into the dark.
Outside the courthouse
A mound shapechanged
Into a trinity of homeless men.

Heedless, she walked on.
Sparks of light broke off the stars
And flew to her fingertips.
She glowed, as if all her lost radiance had returned.
Blues and greens danced over her skin
And the town darkened behind her strange aurora
She shone one last time for him
And for herself, who knows?

He was waiting by the last bridge,
He said his fingers burned
When he touched her. She cried out,
Then her eyes clicked like a box-camera lens.
When he looked in her face
For the ruins of passion
A seal's wide eyes gave the moon back to him.
She jackknifed into the Corrib and held him close
As the sea closed over them.

In the café, they prattle on mobile phones.
'Oh, aren't you taking part?
The theme is the ocean, sea gods, boats.'
Every one is either a mermaid or a near relation
Of Mananaan Mac Lir and someone famous,
Known to the initiated, is playing God.
The whole town has become a showcase and Art
It seems, is all the rage. Meanwhile
Someone is legislating for ugliness.

Next day the parade begins.
The episcopal mermaids slip in
Among the masked figures. The triple-domed big-top
Anchored by the weir is ready for take-off.
The St. Nicholas girls shimmy and sing.
Drums beat, actors just like themselves
Cavort. Could someone recently arrived
Tell the difference between this and real life?

It sweeps down the main streets.
I see houses sliced open like sides of beef,
Their innards indecently exposed
And avenues end abruptly.
This whole masquerade
Could end up with nowhere to go,
Stamping and wailing like a spoilt child.
The river rejects such offerings –
Perhaps in disgust at cheap comparisons –
The carnivals in Venice are stylish.

Only last night, a big machine entered the wrong building
It bulged through the walls of a hotel,
Which burst open, and ran amuck
Scattering kitchen utensils, underwear, guests

Across the grass and into the Corrib. A real mess.
I watched in slow motion and woke up.
Perhaps our dreams contemplate destruction
To stave off madness.

When they reach the Long Walk
The St. Nicholas girls take their leave
One by one and dive in. Nobody notices.

viii

The little mermaids, well-trained convent girls
Have been busy. They have salvaged all
The stained glass windows of the town
And built a cathedral for the marine light.
The Evie Hone above the marble altar
Not so much stolen as saved from desecration
In a pub. Vases of coral and samphire
Are placed before a sunken Spanish Christ.
No luck with candles
Though for incense lumps of ambergris.
The seal woman is amused.
Come, she said, I need a priest.
She gives him air from her mouth,
Watches his mouth opening like a fish.

The place is strewn with pilfered objects from the town.
There are swatches of velvet
Heavy as her first dry breath.
The Kenny's missing baby Jesus
Makes a fat doorstop –
The bold mermaid pats his bottom and he gurgles.
There are three discarded plans for new theatres
And seven hundred Digital computers
With software. Behind her brass bedstead he sees
The clean bones of the unclaimed drowned.
He tries to shout but his voice comes out
Like rusty water from an old tap.
Her great eyes regard him
Dying for her kisses. She obliges.

Soon he notices an easing in his throat.
Gills are forming and a web
Is spreading on his hands and feet.

He'd never understand this woman.
She had loved him before.
Now she ignored him,
The cold bitch. He needed comfort
Or he would go mad in this place.
He was cold and his head ached
From trying to work out
Where things ended and began.
It suited her, this murky definition!

She looks at him, puzzled.
As if some memory flickered,
Like a match going out.
She has no need of him now,
Without fire he is nothing.

She feeds him his portion of air
And bears him to the surface.
A fast ascent – his chest is cracked
Like a walnut. Heart attack –
No, it eases.
She tenses and is gone. She is heading out
Beyond Slyne Head where an island Homer
Is sharking his lyric towards a warmer ocean.

He surfaces at Nimmo's pier.

Back on land, he repossesses his streets,
The sharp plane of block and glass.
Will he surprise us
And walk the shore
Listening for her song?
A ripple of green light
To deepen the clear water of his dreams
Is the best we can hope for.

He heads to Neachtains for a pint of Guinness.

Epilogue

I slip out of the legend
Through a rent in the poem.
Did you think I was talking about my life?
Behind the chi-chi windows of the town
Who knows what goes on.

I must walk home through the frozen streets
And name what stations I can along the way.
The thousand miles I have come
Must be retraced and I must tell out loud
Like prayers the few signposts I have left.
The boatbuilder is dead but what he knew
That was worth knowing floats
In the basin – the boats, blackly beautiful
Will be slow to lie. Their shape, twisted,
Would lose grace and in a storm, sink.

And you, now you have got what you needed
Are you the siren of myth,
Cold and perfected
Or are you sometimes troubled
Like an amputee by phantom pains,
A lunar tug between the hips?

What does it matter?
Poets always conjure and dismiss
Such figures from past or future.
Or a ghost chooses them and leaves
Like that bird fluttering past the panes.
Alone in my room, seasons are changing
I know only this: breath
Alone is not enough.

Occasionally
Stars stream through my body,
I am tidal on the full moon.
When my heels strike the road
Stones give out their tunes –
I would have preferred certainties
But in the tyranny of alternatives
This is better
Than the dried-blood taste of death.